WONDER WOMAN

By Daniel Wallace

INCREDI BUILDS

a division of
INSIGHT ⬤ EDITIONS
San Rafael, California

INTRODUCTION: THE AMAZING AMAZON

SHE IS A PRINCESS OF THEMYSCIRA, THE DAUGHTER OF HIPPOLYTA, AND THE CHAMPION OF THE AMAZONS.

SHE IS THE WARRIOR OF THE GODS AND BEARS THE BLESSINGS AND POWERS OF ATHENA, APHRODITE, HERMES, AND THE ICONS OF THE GREEK PANTHEON.

SHE IS THE CHOSEN ENVOY TO MAN'S WORLD, A FRIEND TO ETTA CANDY AND STEVE TREVOR, AND A TIRELESS AMBASSADOR FOR GLOBAL PEACE.

SHE IS A FIERCE FOE TO HER ENEMIES AND THOSE WHO THREATEN THE INNOCENT, WHETHER SHE IS STANDING ALONE OR ALONGSIDE HER ALLIES IN THE JUSTICE LEAGUE.

SHE IS DIANA. SHE IS WONDER WOMAN.

FOR MORE THAN SEVENTY-FIVE YEARS, Wonder Woman has served as a cornerstone of the DC Comics universe and an inspiration to fans across the globe. Created by psychologist William Moulton Marston, Wonder Woman was one of the only female comic-book superheroes when she debuted in the pages of *All-Star Comics* #8 in 1941, and for decades she helped expand the definition of inclusiveness in popular culture.

The character has starred on television in the 1970s and in movie theaters during the 2010s, but none of it could have happened without thousands of stories and decades of comics. Wonder Woman is one of the only DC heroes (the others being Superman and Batman) who have remained in near-continuous publication since their debut in the Golden Age during the 1930s and 1940s. For this reason, the character has been enshrined as a cornerstone hero in the DC Universe and one of the most significant cultural creations of the past century.

Her long history in comics has seen her team up with Superman and Batman during World War II, undergo bizarre romantic entanglements with bird-men and aliens during the 1950s, and briefly become a white-suited martial artist during the mod 1960s. More recent tales have found success by exploring Wonder Woman's ties to Greek mythology and pitting her against the armies of Ares or the terrors of gorgons and minotaurs.

No challenge is too tough for Wonder Woman to tackle, and no person is beneath her notice. Though she is famous as an embodiment of female accomplishment, Wonder Woman is ultimately a hero for everyone.

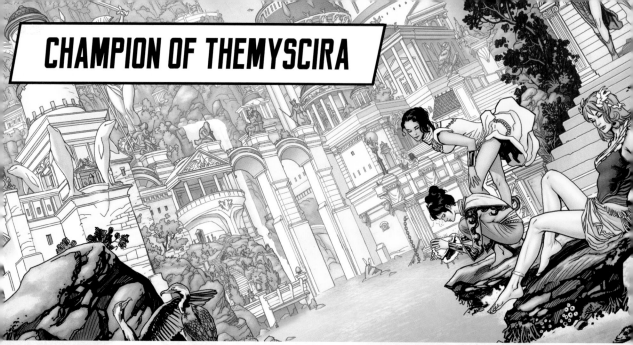

CHAMPION OF THEMYSCIRA

WONDER WOMAN IS AN AMAZON,
a member of an all-female race of warriors who
inhabit the hidden island of Themyscira, or
Paradise Island. The near-immortal Amazons
have built an ideal society under the leadership of
Queen Hippolyta, in which education, physical
fitness, and sisterly bonds are prized above all else.

Known to her Amazon sisters as Diana,
Wonder Woman is the daughter of the queen. She
carries the noble birthright of a Themysciran princess. Though her mother initially forbade Diana
from participating in the contest to determine
which Amazon would become their champion,
Diana refused to remain on the sidelines. After
putting on a disguise, she won the battle and
earned the right to call herself Wonder Woman.

The Amazons remained isolated on Themyscira
for thousands of years until the arrival of a US Air
Force pilot named Steve Trevor prompted Diana to
venture forth into Man's World.

YOU SEE, GIRLS, THERE'S NOTHING TO IT - ALL YOU HAVE TO DO IS HAVE CONFIDENCE IN YOUR OWN STRENGTH!

5A

- HIGH RESISTANCE TO MOST FORMS OF PHYSICAL DAMAGE
- FLIGHT

- SUPERHUMAN STRENGTH

- ACCELERATED HEALING
- AMAZON TRAINING IN THE ARTS OF ATHLETICS, ARMED AND UNARMED COMBAT, AND BATTLEFIELD STRATEGY

WITH HER KEEN AMAZON EAR **WONDER WOMAN** CLEARLY HEARS THE LAWYER'S VOICE TELEPHONING IN THE NEXT ROOM.

WHAT! GREAT HEAVENS, VINA, YOU SAY BYRON GRANT IS THERE TO SEE YOU?

4

- SUPERHUMAN SPEED AND AGILITY
- HEIGHTENED SENSES

2

YOU CAN *STAND* HERE IF YOU LIKE, JAY, BUT I'M GOING TO DO SOMETHING, AND I CAN'T DO IT AS YEOMAN PRINCE --

ROBOT PLANE -- COME QUICKLY!

AND, IN ANSWER TO THE AMAZING AMAZON'S TELEPATHIC COMMAND, AN INVISIBLE PLANE STREAKS FROM THE TWILIGHT SKY --

Wonder Woman sometimes uses the secret identity of Diana Prince, allowing her to travel incognito and make it easier to study the customs of the outside world.

GIFTS OF THE GODS

According to some tales, Wonder Woman's abilities come from the gods themselves.

- *DEMETER*, THE GODDESS OF AGRICULTURE AND FERTILITY, GAVE DIANA STRENGTH AND HEALING.
- *ATHENA*, THE GODDESS OF WISDOM, GAVE DIANA HER SHARP MIND AND HER GIFT FOR STRATEGY.
- *ARTEMIS*, THE GODDESS OF THE HUNT AND THE MOON, GAVE DIANA ENHANCED SENSES AND EMPATHY WITH ANIMALS.
- *HESTIA*, THE GODDESS OF THE HEARTH, GAVE DIANA HER INVULNERABILITY TO FIRE.
- *HERMES*, THE MESSENGER GOD, GAVE DIANA THE POWERS OF SPEED AND FLIGHT.
- *APHRODITE*, THE GODDESS OF LOVE, GAVE DIANA HER BEAUTY AND HER CARING HEART.

Who is she?

WHERE does she come from? How did she obtain her human, yet invincible abilities?

These are the questions everyone is asking — for WONDER WOMAN has become the talk of the hour all over America!

With the beauty of Aphrodite, the wisdom of Athena, the strength of Hercules and the speed of Mercury, this glamorous Amazon Princess flashes vividly across America's horizon from that mysterious Paradise Isle, where women rule supreme

GEAR OF THE GODS

THE AMAZONS TRAINED DIANA in the arts of hunting and fighting, but Wonder Woman also possesses special equipment to make her adventuring even more successful.

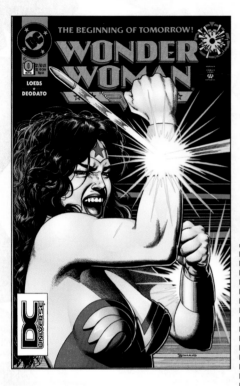

BRACELETS

Wonder Woman's indestructible bracelets were formed from the Aegis, a legendary shield once carried by the goddess Athena. Wonder Woman can tap into the speed of Hermes, moving her arms quickly enough to intercept bullets with her bracelets and deflect them harmlessly. When she faces bigger threats, Wonder Woman can cross her wrists and slam both bracelets together in an X shape—an act that releases a devastating wave of energy.

TIARA

Wonder Woman's tiara has razor-sharp edges and bears a red star that indicates Diana's status as a champion. The tiara travels in a curving arc when thrown and returns to Wonder Woman's hand like a boomerang.

LASSO OF TRUTH

Always worn at Wonder Woman's hip, the golden Lariat of Hestia is a symbol of Diana's commitment to the principles of truth and justice. This unbreakable magical artifact forces any living being it touches to respond truthfully to any question.

ARMOR

Worn only during ceremonial events or in preparation for particularly perilous battles, Wonder Woman's armor bears her double-*W* insignia and incorporates the majestic wings of a golden eagle.

SWORD AND SHIELD

Wonder Woman's sturdy short sword carries the blessings of the gods. Her round shield is compact and durable, allowing Wonder Woman to swing it firmly as a bashing weapon.

INVISIBLE PLANE

One of Wonder Woman's most recognizable accessories, the invisible plane, has been part of her legend since her earliest appearances. It can vanish from sight at Wonder Woman's command, allowing for stealth attacks or the ability to park it in plain sight without attracting the attention of gawkers.

PURPLE RAY

This mystery of Amazon science is used on the island of Themyscira to accomplish a number of remarkable effects. Most commonly, purple ray energies are harnessed into exotic devices that are then used to heal wounds and cure fatal diseases.

FEARSOME FOES

BECAUSE WONDER WOMAN IS A PROUD Amazon, many of her most dangerous enemies are figures from ancient myth. But as soon as Diana made her mark in Man's World, she began to attract a new host of foes—all with their own reasons to hate Wonder Woman and all she stands for!

THE CHEETAH

Barbara Ann Minerva, a former archaeologist, fell under a terrible curse. She gained catlike reflexes, slashing claws, and uncontrollable bloodlust. When she is able to escape the Cheetah's influence and control her transformation, Barbara is actually one of Diana's close friends.

GIGANTA

Doris Zuel possesses the power to grow to colossal size, gaining proportional strength and resistance to injury in the process.

THE BARONESS, OPENING THE CELL DOOR STEALTHILY WITH A SKELETON KEY, THROWS THE MAGIC LASSO OVER *WONDER WOMAN*.

AT LAST I'VE GOT YOU! COME WITH ME!

I—I MUST OBEY YOU! THE MAGIC LASSO COMPELS ME!

BARONESS

Baroness Paula Von Gunther was one of Wonder Woman's earliest foes when the superhero made her debut during the 1940s. Originally a spy for the Nazi regime, the Baroness also pursued an interest in the occult that put her in possession of dangerous mystical knowledge.

DOCTOR PSYCHO

One of the most powerful telepaths on Earth, Edgar Cizko, aka Doctor Psycho, can read minds, control the actions of others, and cause his victims to suffer from terrifying, nightmarish hallucinations.

CIRCE

The immortal sorceress Circe has near-complete control over matter and is able to change humans into pigs with a snap of her fingers.

ARES

The legendary Greek god of war, Ares has existed for many thousands of years as the personification of armed conflict. He can take many forms, but he typically appears as a glowering figure clad in full battle armor.

FIRST BORN

As the original child of Zeus and Hera, the god known only as the First Born seeks to claim the throne of Olympus and won't let anyone stand in his way.

MEDUSA

Medusa, the Queen of Monsters, is a Gorgon with snakes for hair and the ability to turn anyone to stone if they gaze into her eyes.

TRUSTED ALLIES

WONDER WOMAN MAKES FRIENDS wherever she goes. Her allies are endless, both on Themyscira and in the wider world. A few figures, however, hold special places in Diana's heart.

STEVE TREVOR

US Air Force Pilot Steve Trevor accidentally crashed on Paradise Island. As the first man to set foot on Themyscira in ages, Steve was initially out of his element, but he recovered quickly when charged with introducing Diana to the modern world. Through it all, he has shared an on-again, off-again romantic connection with Wonder Woman.

DONNA TROY

When Wonder Woman rescued the young Donna Troy from a building fire, she brought the orphaned girl to be raised on Themyscira. Donna became Diana's "little sister" and eventually joined the Teen Titans under the identity of Wonder Girl.

ETTA CANDY

Gifted with an irrepressible spirit, Etta Candy is always ready with a witty come-back. Over the years, Etta has played a number of roles, from the ringleader of the "Holliday Girls" at the Holliday College for Women, to an Air Force captain and high-ranking intelligence officer.

CASSIE SANDSMARK

The second Wonder Girl after Donna Troy, Cassie Sandsmark is the daughter of an archaeologist who received her powers from magical Greek relics. She is a longtime member of the Teen Titans and has a mysterious connection to Zeus, the king of the Greek gods.

ARTEMIS

Artemis is the champion of the Egyptian Bana-Mighdall Amazons. Artemis even briefly took over Diana's role as Wonder Woman during the 1990s!

HIPPOLYTA

Diana's mother, Hippolyta, is queen of the Amazons of Themyscira. She has lived for thousands of years and views the safety of her people as her most important duty.

TEAM AFFILIATIONS

Though Wonder Woman is a formidable warrior, she is even more powerful when she teams up with others.

- **THE JUSTICE LEAGUE:** WONDER WOMAN IS A FOUNDING MEMBER OF THIS ELITE SUPER-TEAM ALONGSIDE SUPERMAN, BATMAN, GREEN LANTERN, AQUAMAN, CYBORG, AND THE FLASH.

- **THE JUSTICE SOCIETY:** WONDER WOMAN AND THE JUSTICE SOCIETY FOUGHT THE AGGRESSORS OF THE AXIS POWERS DURING WORLD WAR II.

- **AMAZONS OF THEMYSCIRA:** THE AMAZONS STAYED ISOLATED FOR THOUSANDS OF YEARS, DEVELOPING CLOSE-KNIT BONDS THAT UNITE EVERY SISTER ON PARADISE ISLAND. WONDER WOMAN HOLDS A SPECIAL STATUS AMONG THE AMAZONS, BEING BOTH THEIR PRINCESS AND THE COMBAT CHAMPION WHO WON THE RIGHT TO VISIT MAN'S WORLD.

- **GREEK PANTHEON:** DIANA HAS LONG HAD A RUMORED CONNECTION TO THE BLOODLINE OF ZEUS, AND AT ONE POINT SHE EVEN TOOK OVER ARES'S ROLE AS THE GOD OF WAR.

WONDER WOMAN DEBUTED IN THE pages of *All-Star Comics* #8 in 1941, during the era of comics now known as the Golden Age. Superman and Batman had debuted only a few years earlier in the pages of *Action Comics* and *Detective Comics*, respectively, and Wonder Woman was a new and exciting addition to the growing genre of the superhero.

In a genre dominated by male characters, Wonder Woman's gender made her stand out—but that wasn't the only remarkable thing about her. Her creator, William Moulton Marston, was a psychologist and inventor—a far cry from the sci-fi and crime writers who dominated the emerging medium. With his wife, Elizabeth Holloway Marston, Marston sought to create a new kind of costumed hero—one who would prioritize love and understanding over punches and kicks.

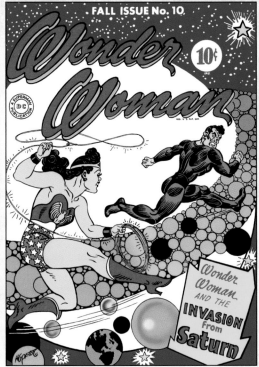

Artist H. G. Peter illustrated Wonder Woman's first comic-book story: a nine-page tale in the back pages of *All-Star Comics* #8 (December 1941). The character received cover billing on 1942's *Sensation Comics* #1, and shortly thereafter she won the right to headline her own ongoing *Wonder Woman* comic-book series.

Marston and Peter wasted no time in introducing elements that would come to define Wonder Woman for decades, including her origins as an Amazon on Paradise Island, her romantic interest in US Air Force Pilot Steve Trevor, and even her famous Lasso of Truth. This last may have been inspired by Marston's real-life invention of the systolic blood pressure test, a key component of the lie-detecting polygraph machine.

The creative innovations kept on coming throughout the Golden Age, with stories involving an Amazon rodeo on giant kangaroos and an invisible airplane made from the mysterious substance Amazsilikon. The Wonder Woman of this era defended the world against Queen Flamina and her sun warriors and fought "tigeapes" when a chunk of Neptunia crashed into the Pacific Ocean.

But newsstands in the 1940s had become crowded with superheroes as publishers tried to ride the wave that Superman, Batman, and Wonder Woman had created.

Though Wonder Woman comics continued to sell, the abrupt cancellation of once-popular titles starring the Flash, Green Lantern, and others seemed to indicate a need for a storytelling shakeup—lest the Amazing Amazon suffer the same fate.

The tone of Wonder Woman's adventures would shift dramatically in the 1950s, ushering in what would be known as the Silver Age of Comics.

THE SILVER AGE

WITH SALES NUMBERS
suggesting waning interest in the
superhero genre, Wonder Woman,
alongside Superman and Batman,
was one of the few costumed heroes
to remain in continuous publication.
Romance comics were on the
upswing at the time, and Wonder
Woman's relationship with Steve
Trevor seemed like fertile ground
for teasing "will they or won't they"
plots centered on hurt feelings and
marriage proposals. Alongside Steve
Trevor's new prominence, a host of
newcomers popped up to seek Diana's
hand in marriage.

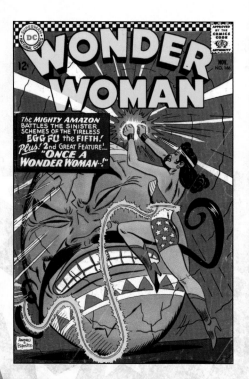

The Silver Age ran from the 1950s through the late 1960s, a period in which second-generation writers and artists frequently took the reins from the original creative teams. The Silver Age also bore the effects of the Comics Code, a 1954 mandate banning excessive violence and sexual innuendo. In Wonder Woman's comic, new supporting characters and crazy villains, from Egg Fu to the Glop, appeared during a time when no idea seemed too far-fetched to appear on the comic page.

Flashback stories set during Diana's upbringing on Paradise Island resulted in the introduction of Wonder Girl and Wonder Tot—de-aged versions of Diana that, at least in the case of Wonder Girl, later became separate characters in their own right.

In 1960's milestone issue #28 of *The Brave and the Bold*, Wonder Woman united with other prominent heroes to defeat the extraterrestrial invader Starro and form the Justice League of America. But as America entered a countercultural revolution at the tail end of the '60s, Wonder Woman faced a need to change with the times.

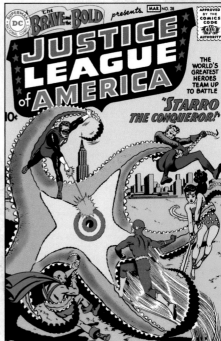

CHANGING TIMES

THE BRONZE AGE OF COMICS
took root in the late 1960s and reflected
the societal changes sweeping the nation by
focusing on cultural issues and equal rights.

Wonder Woman severed her ties to the
Amazons and resigned from the Justice
League of America, seeking tutelage under
the wise master I-Ching to become a non-su-
perpowered martial artist. Wonder Woman's
iconic costume was also retired, and Diana
developed a taste for mod fashion and
memorably donned an all-white jumpsuit.

Wonder Woman pursued many new roles
during this era, becoming a translator for the
United Nations and even an astronaut for
NASA. A 1973 issue sought to acknowledge
the cultural conversation on race when it
introduced Nubia—a dark-skinned Amazon
who sought validation in the combat arena.

By the mid-1970s, Wonder Woman had
ditched her mod getup and returned to her
classic appearance—just in time for a new
resurgence. A live-action *Wonder Woman*
television show debuted in 1975, starring
Lynda Carter as the amazing Amazon.
Suddenly, the character was more famous
than ever.

But while Wonder Woman had returned
to something comfortable and familiar,
DC Comics had big plans for its fictional
universe. Massive changes were coming for
Wonder Woman—and soon.

THE MODERN AGE

THE BRONZE AGE ENDED WITH the destruction of a multiverse. *Crisis on Infinite Earths* was a twelve-part comic-book miniseries that chronicled a reality-altering event that wiped clean nearly fifty years of history. In the new, sleeker continuity, heroes like Wonder Woman started anew from square one.

Wonder Woman's self-titled series came to an end with issue #329, and a rebooted *Wonder Woman* monthly comic launched with a new issue #1 in 1987. Writer/artist George Perez and co-plotter Greg Potter drew heavily on Greek mythology to tell a new legend of the champion of the Amazons. This version of Diana, slow to anger but unstoppable in battle, sought to bring peace to the world.

The *Wonder Woman* series took some unexpected turns during the '90s. Diana put in hours as a minimum-wage worker at Taco Whiz. Artemis, an edgy Amazon with a taste for combat, joined the cast in 1994 as reader tastes turned toward "extreme" heroes with take-no-prisoners attitudes.

In a short-lived storyline, Artemis became the new Wonder Woman, and Diana temporarily donned biker-girl togs to continue the fight.

The *Wonder Woman* series enjoyed an influential run by writer Greg Rucka during the early 2000s, with Wonder Woman facing attacks from Doctor Psycho, Veronica Cale, and the Silver Swan. The character even received her own original graphic novel, *Wonder Woman: The Hiketeia*, in 2002.

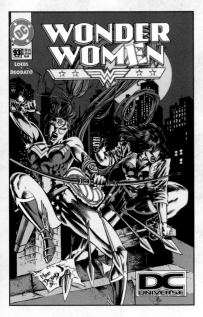

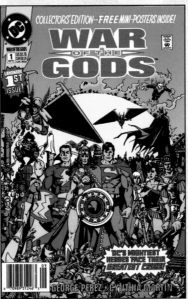

In 2010, the *Wonder Woman* series returned to its original numbering in order to hit the six-hundred-issue milestone. The issue featured a redesigned black-pants costume by artist Jim Lee with input by writer J. Michael Straczynski.

As the next decade took hold, Wonder Woman stood in a position of prominence as one of the most famous and influential heroes of popular culture. But DC Comics had another reboot planned. This event, "The New 52," would end the run of every current comic and replace them with new #1 issues from fifty-two brand-new series. *Wonder Woman*, of course, was one of the first titles to set the new tone.

THE ATTENTION-GRABBING "New 52" relaunch allowed *Wonder Woman* writer Brian Azzarello and artist Cliff Chiang to put their own spin on a character whose origins had already undergone significant revamping. In this interpretation, Diana was the demigod offspring of Hippolyta and Zeus. Steve Trevor was now a high-ranking government agent acting as Wonder Woman's liaison, and he soon found himself nursing an unrequited crush on the new hero.

Diana was also a member of the Justice League in the "New 52" and thwarted a planetary invasion by the armies of Darkseid. It wasn't long before romance blossomed between Wonder Woman and her teammate Superman.

The most recent changes to Wonder Woman's backstory came about as part of DC Comics' "Rebirth" event in 2016.

And in 2017, the character reached her biggest audience to date when she premiered in movie theaters across the globe in the *Wonder Woman* feature film, portrayed by Gal Gadot.

THE COSTUMES OF A CHAMPION

WONDER WOMAN'S COSTUME is timeless, famous, and iconic. Though it has undergone tweaks in the decades since its first appearance in 1941, the costume has always retained its most recognizable elements.

1

THE ORIGINAL

Wonder Woman's first costume resembled the American flag. Designed by artist H. G. Peter and writer William Moulton Marston, this costume and its minor variants—including bottom-half revisions alternating between shorts and a skirt—remained in use throughout the Golden and Silver Ages of comic-book publishing.

2

THE '70S

Wonder Woman won new fame during this decade with a live-action television series as well as her Saturday-morning appearances on the animated series *Super Friends*. Her costume, now a body suit, took on a simplified, streamlined look that many regard as the definitive Wonder Woman outfit.

POST-CRISIS

3

In the wake of the comic-book miniseries *Crisis on Infinite Earths*, writer/artist George Pérez gave Wonder Woman a 1987 redesign. She now sported fuller hair and heel-less boots, and a "WW" logo—originally designed in the early '80s—replaced the eagle symbol.

COVERUP

Artist Jim Lee gave Wonder Woman pants for the first time in 2010.

5

6

NEW 52

DC Comics rebooted its universe with the "New 52" initiative in 2011.

CONTEMPORARY

For a brief time in the mid-'90s, Diana surrendered the mantle of Wonder Woman to her rival, Artemis. Artist Mike Deodato introduced a modernized replacement costume designed by Brian Bolland, which retained a "WW" logo and a few familiar stars but incorporated biking shorts and an open jacket.

4

7

REBIRTH

In 2016, Wonder Woman received a Greek-inspired upgrade. Incorporating a leather skirt and bringing back the eagle design, this costume was similar to the one worn by Gal Gadot in Wonder Woman's cinematic debut, 2016's *Batman v Superman: Dawn of Justice.*

WONDER WOMAN'S MOST MEMORABLE ADVENTURES

SENSATION COMICS (VOL. 1) #1

Wonder Woman journeys to the outside world in this origin tale, which introduces its main character as "a woman with the eternal beauty of Aphrodite" who also possesses "the steel sinews of a Hercules."

WONDER WOMAN (VOL. 1) #107

Taking her cue from the popular *Superboy* comic, the amazing Amazon experiences a flashback to her youth. As the soon-to-be Wonder Girl, the teenaged Diana undergoes a series of trials on Paradise Island to earn the right to wear her costume.

WONDER WOMAN (VOL. 1) #178-180

An all-new era begins in this late '60s Wonder Woman epic, which digs deep into hippie slang and flower-power iconography. Diana, having renounced her Amazon powers and retired her Wonder Woman identity, opens a mod clothing boutique and studies martial arts under the blind master I-Ching.

WONDER WOMAN (VOL. 1) #212-222

When Diana eventually reclaimed her Wonder Woman identity, the comics papered over her martial-artist escapades by introducing a convenient bout of amnesia.

WONDER WOMAN (VOL. 2) #90-93

Queen Hippolyta calls for a contest to elect a new champion of the Amazons. The contestants include current champion Diana as well as Artemis, stern warrior of the breakaway Bana-Mighdall tribe.

WONDER WOMAN (VOL. 2) #1

Wonder Woman's continuity is reset to the beginning with this all-new monthly series and first issue.

WONDER WOMAN: REBIRTH #1

As part of a company-wide focus on the essential qualities of the core heroes of DC Comics, Wonder Woman stars in this standalone issue that attempts to reconcile the character's reboots and origin stories.

CONCLUSION: WONDER WOMAN'S LEGACY

Wonder Woman is both a champion of peace and a symbol of bravery. She is a feminist icon who has conquered multiple mediums while staying relevant to the concerns of today.

No matter what she faces, Wonder Woman never stops fighting. Her idealism lights the way to a better and more equitable future for us all.

MAKE IT YOUR OWN

One of the great things about IncrediBuilds™ models is that each one is completely customizable. The untreated natural wood can be decorated with paints, pencils, pens, beads, sequins—the list goes on and on!

Feel free to unleash your creative genius as you customize your model. Start by coming up with an idea for your model. Anything goes! You can also follow the craft ideas here to make something totally incredible!

For this model, how you decorate it depends on what materials you choose. If you are using paints, paint it after it's fully assembled. If you're using colored pencils, you'll want to draw and color *before* you assemble the model.

CLASSIC GOLDEN AGE: GOLD AND RED

Wonder Woman won the hearts of fans everywhere when she first jumped on the scene in 1942. Wonder Woman has outlasted many of her contemporaries to become the bombastic superhero we know her as today. It's only fitting to showcase her iconic tiara as it first appeared in the Golden Age of comics.

WHAT YOU NEED:

- Paints (yellow and red)
- Paintbrush

1. Paint the whole model—except for the star—yellow. You will probably need two coats. Let each coat dry before adding another.
2. Paint the star red.

NEW 52 DESIGN

The "New 52" dramatically rebooted the entire DC Universe, and with that reboot came some stellar uniform changes. Wonder Woman herself was given a whole new look, sporting a sleek silver tiara rather than the traditional gold.

WHAT YOU NEED:

- Paints (gray, silver, and red)
- Paintbrush

1. Start by painting the entire model—except for the star—gray. This will allow the silver paint to shine brighter and more opaquely. Let dry.
2. Paint the entire model—except for the star—silver.
3. Paint the star red.

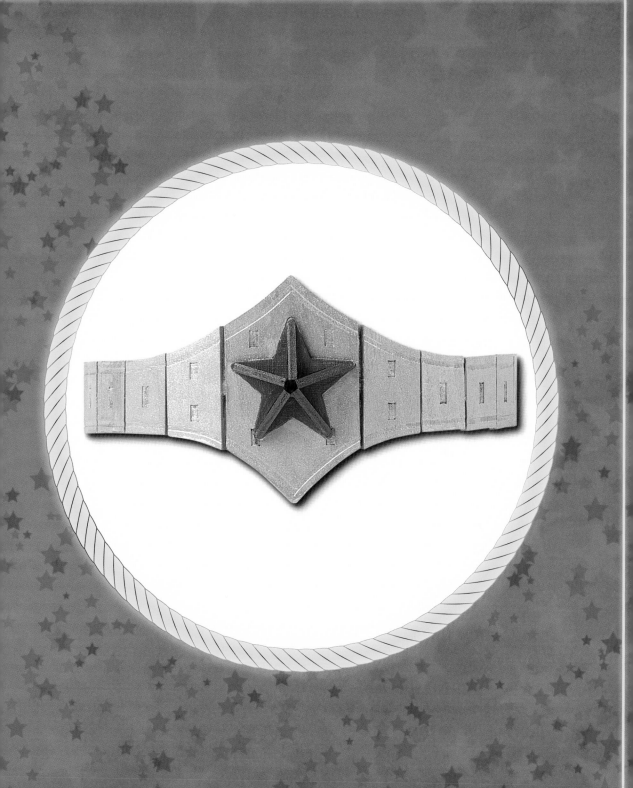

WONDER WOMAN UNIFORM

Wonder Woman has had many costume changes over her seventy-five years of publication. However, she will always be known by her red and gold corset top and star-spangled blue briefs. This project pays homage to the classic, the one and only, Wonder Woman.

WHAT YOU NEED:

- Paints (metallic gold, red, and blue)
- Gold embroidery floss
- Star rhinestones
- Glue
- Toothpick

WHAT YOU MIGHT WANT:

- Tweezers

1. Start by painting the mid-section of the tiara in blue.
2. Follow the engravings to line the edges and paint the back of the tiara gold.
3. Paint the star red.

STAR RHINESTONES

1. Use a toothpick to put a drop of glue where you want a sparkly star.
2. Carefully place the star on top of the glue drop.
3. Repeat as you add stars.

LASSO OF TRUTH

1. Cut two lengths of gold embroidery floss about 20 inches long.
2. Tie together on one end and tape that end to a flat surface.
3. Twist and turn each length over the other making a rope braid.
4. When the length is what you want, tie off the ends in a knot.
5. Glue one of the knots to the inside of the tiara. Let dry.
6. Twist the rope into position and glue into place.
7. Finish by gluing the end knot to the inside of the tiara.